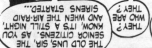

THERE'LL BE BLUE BIRDS OVER

January 11, 1968

BUT IT CAN'T BE LUCRETIA, RUFUS. HOW WOULD SHE KNOW WE LIVED HERE?

I DON'T KNOW, BUT IT'S HER

'ULLO, FLOOKY-BOY. NICE PAD YOU'VE GOT 'ERE

BUT, LUCRETIA, HOW DID YOU KNOW WHERE TO COME—AND COME TO THAT, WHY HAVE YOU COME?

WELL, I 'AD ME TOIL 'N' TROUBLE TRANSISTOR TUNED IN, DIDN'T I? AN' JUST AFTER I'D TURNED THAT GEEZER INTO A TOAD...

OF COURSE, FLOOK. YOU SAID YOU'D LIKE TO CONGRATULATE LUCRETIA, DON'T YOU REMEMBER?

SO I DID, BUT I DON'T SEE HOW LUCRETIA PICKED ME UP

ANYONE WIV MISCHIEF IN THEIR 'EARTS COMES OVER, FLOOKY-BOY. NOW WHAT IS IT? AS YOU KNOW I'M ALWAYS READY FOR A WICKED GIGGLE

DO YOU MEAN TO SAY LUCRETIA THAT IF ANYONE THINKS WICKED THOUGHTS YOU CAN HEAR THEM ON YOUR TRANSISTOR?

FIFTY-MILE RADIUS ONLY. BUT YEAH. GREATEST INVENTION SINCE THE PRESSURE CAULDRON

USED TO 'AVE TER LUG AROUND ME CRYSTAL BALL SET, DIDN'T I? SLOWED YOU DOWN DIABOLICAL

I CAN HARDLY BELIEVE IT

'AVE A LISTEN THEN

ANOTHER BABY CHAM, DARLING? COURSE EET WON'T 'URT YOW......'ERE DORIS, SLIP ANOTHER DOUBLE VODKA IN EET

WELL, IT WAS NICE OF YOU TO DROP IN, BUT I'M OVER MY BAD THOUGHTS NOW. SO...

IF YOU CALLS IN A WITCH, FLOOKY-BOY. YOU CALLS IN A WITCH I AINT GOIN' TILL I'VE DONE SOMEFING WICKED TO SOMEONE—EVEN IF IT'S YOU!

YOU MEAN YOU'VE GOT TO CAST A SPELL NOW I'VE CALLED YOU IN?

UNION RULES, I'N'T IT? NOW, WHAT'S ON YER MIND?

OH, VERY WELL, BUT I DON'T WANT IT TO BE TOO STRONG, YOU SEE. NOTHING DRASTIC

I COULDN'T DO NUFFINK TOO DIABOLICAL EVEN IF I WANTED TO. YOUR THOUGHTS WEREN'T WICKED ENOUGH

OH, IN THAT CASE... WELL, THE PEOPLE HERE HAVE BEEN VERY UNPLEASANT TO ME JUST BECAUSE I'M SHORT AND FURRY—

THEY WOULDN'T LET HIM IN THEIR CLUB, AND THEY LIT A FIERY CROSS IN THE GARDEN...

AND THEY TRIED TO PATRONISE ME, AND THEY INSULTED ME

I GET YER. RIGHT THEN, WHERE'S THE KITCHEN?

FLOOK FOR A NEIGHBOUR

July 10, 1965

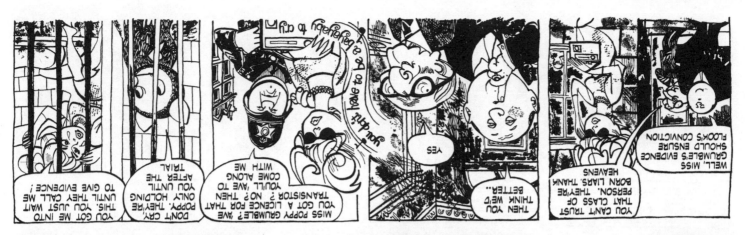

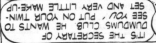

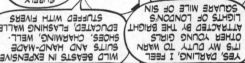

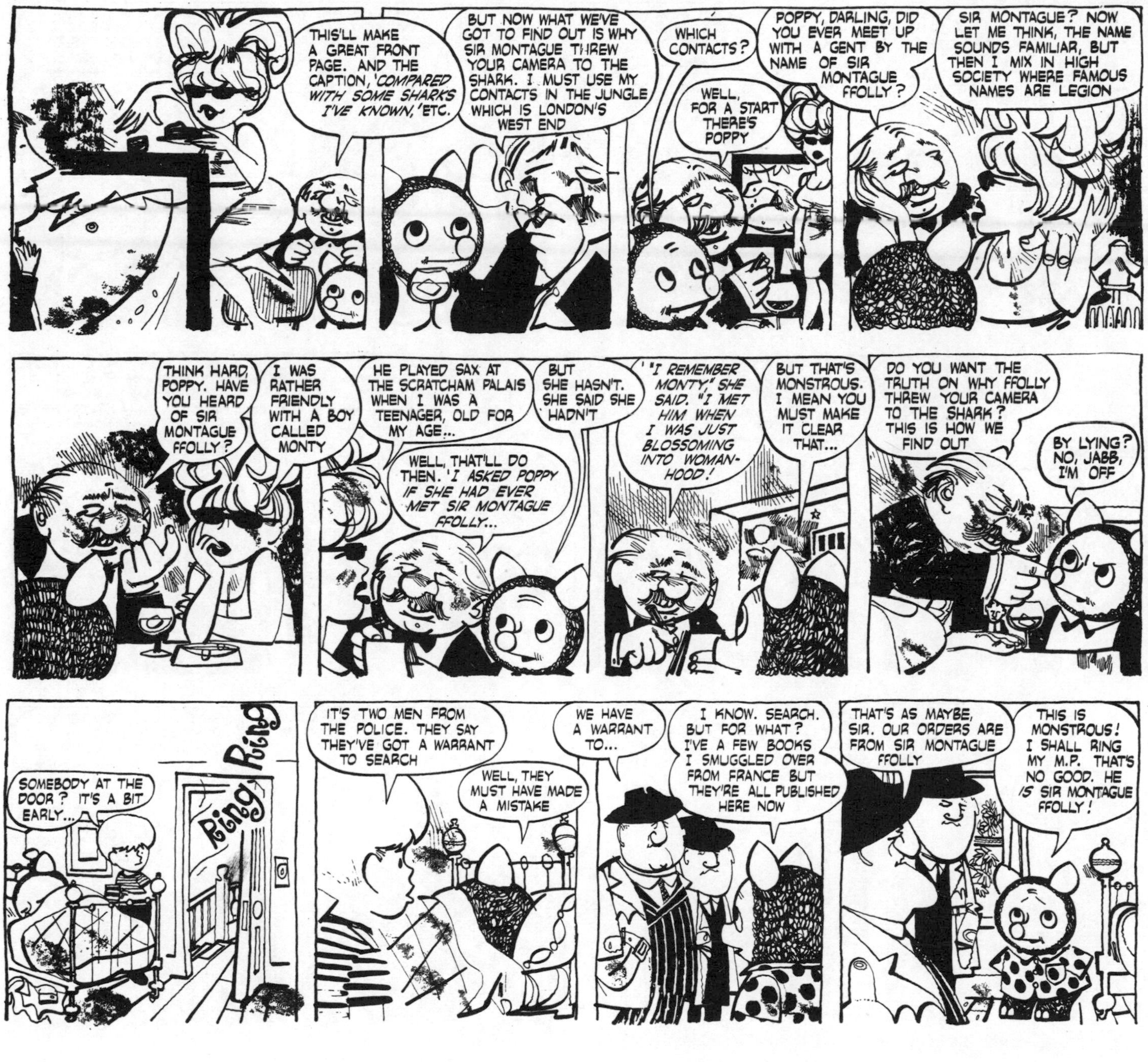

THE CLIP-ON-BOW-TIE AFFAIR
July 24, 1963

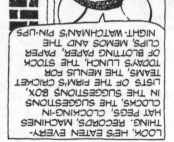

A SAD DAY, THIS. OUR REGIMENT HAS FOUGHT WITH HONOUR AT WATERLOO, MALPLAQUET AND DURIN' THE GENERAL STRIKE, BUT TOMORROW WE BECOME PART OF THE PIONEER CORPS

LOOK! ALL THE SOLDIERS ARE CRYING

YES, TOMORROW WE BECOME PART OF A SHOWER WHOSE OFFICERS DROP THEIR AITCHES. WHAT? WHAT?

I BET HE DOES WHEN HE TALKS ABOUT HUNTING

AND OUR MASCOT, DEAR OLD PONGO, IS TO GO. WAR OFFICE ORDERS. 'TO BE DESTROYED, ONE GOAT, REGIMENTAL MASCOT OF THE ISLE OF WIGHT GUARDS.' PONGO' ONE OF US!

I DON'T SEE WHAT WE CAN DO. IT'S NO GOOD PRETENDING TO BE MEMBERS OF THE R.S.P.C.A. THEY'D PROBABLY PASS A MOTION IN FAVOUR OF GOAT-SHOOTING

VOLUNTEERS FOR THE FIRING PARTY! YOU, YOU, (SOB) AND YOU

GOODBYE, PONGO OLD THING

IF EVER A GOAT DESERVED AN 'EAVEN FULL OF TIN CANS PONGO DO

FIRE!

FUNNY THE OFFICER SHOUTED, 'FIRE!', AND THERE WERE NO SHOTS

WHY DON'T YOU LOOK, FLOOK?

SAR'NT, WHY DIDN'T THE MEN FIRE WHEN I GAVE THE ORDER? MUTINY, YOU KNOW. SERIOUS CHARGE. REFUSIN' TO SHOOT A GOAT AT THE COMMAND, 'FIRE'

THEY SAYS THEY CAN'T, SIR. NOT OLD PONGO. IT'S NOT AS IF 'E WAS A 'UMAN BEING

VERY WELL THEN, I SHALL HAVE TO DESPATCH HIM WITH MY SWORD

EVEN WORSE. I'LL HAVE TO COVER MY EYES AGAIN

SO WILL I

NO, I CAN'T DO IT, EITHER. EVEN THOUGH I CAN'T SEE HIM I CAN SMELL HIM. TOO MANY MEMORIES

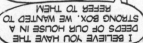

FLOOK, WHY ARE YOU WEARING A BOWLER HAT?

BECAUSE WE ARE GOING TO THE CITY TO GRAPPLE WITH OUR LAWYERS!

HERE WE ARE — 'PILFAH, PILFAH, ROBB, STEEL AND PILFAH'

THEY CAN'T BE VERY SUCCESSFUL LAWYERS, CAN THEY, FLOOK? I MEAN, IT'S A VERY SHABBY, OLD HOUSE

ON THE CONTRARY. LAWYERS ARE LIKE TAILORS AND WINE MERCHANTS. THE DUSTIER THE PREMISES THE MORE SOLID THE ESTABLISHMENT

AH, HERE WE ARE. IT SAYS, 'KNOCK AND WAIT'. FUNNY — DOESN'T SEEM TO BE ANYONE HERE

CAN'T YOU GENTLEMEN READ? 'KNOCK AND WAIT'. IT SAYS. ALWAYS HAS. ALWAYS WILL

WE DID KNOCK FOR AGES, AND WAITED FOR A LONG TIME AND THEN KNOCKED AGAIN

EH, EH? DON'T MUMBLE. CAN'T HEAR A WORD YOU'RE SAYIN'. WHAT D'YER WANT, EH, EH?

I SAID... OH, NEVER MIND. DEAF AS A POST

WHO DID YER WANT TO SEE, EH?

WELL, IT DOESN'T REALLY...

PILFAH, PILFAH, ROBB, STEEL & PILFAH

YER CAN'T SEE OLD MR. PILFAH — HE ISN'T IN TODAY, YER SEE

WELL, IT DOESN'T MATTER. WHAT ABOUT YOUNG MR. PILFAH?

MR. ROBB DID YER SAY? IN COURT. IN COURT, YER SEE

NO, NO! YOUNG MR. PILFAH. YOUNG MR. PILFAH!

MR. STEEL? WENT DOWN ON THE TITANIC. TRAGIC BUSINESS. PERHAPS YOU'D BETTER SEE YOUNG MR. PILFAH

COR. MADE IT!

IT'S A GOOD THING WE'RE GOING TO SEE YOUNG MR. PILFAH. HE'S SURE TO BE A LITTLE MORE GO-AHEAD THAN THE REST OF THE PLACE

YES, IF EVERYBODY HERE IS AS OLD AS THE CLERK IT MUST TAKE AGES AND AGES TO GET ANYTHING DONE

THAT'S THE WHOLE POINT. THE LONGER IT TAKES THE MORE IT COSTS. MOST LAWYERS TAKE A COURSE IN SENILITY

WELL, WHY DO WE USE THIS FIRM?

FAMILY LAWYERS ARE SIMPLY PEOPLE WHO REMEMBER ONE'S GREAT GRANDFATHER. THEY DON'T HAVE TO GET THINGS DONE

YOUNG MASTER PILFAH WILL RECEIVE YOU NOW

WELL, WHAT IS IT? SOME SHARES? A SEAT ON THE BOARD? A LUXURY TRIP FOR TWO TO THE WEST INDIES? YOU NAME IT — WE'LL GET IT YOU

NO, IT'S MUCH LESS THAN THAT. I WANT TO KNOW *WHAT IS INSTANT SLUDGE FOR?*

WHAT DID YOU ASK, FLOOK? I MUST BE GOING MAD. PERHAPS I NEED A LONG REST

I SIMPLY ASKED, 'WHAT *IS INSTANT SLUDGE FOR?*'

YES, THAT'S WHAT I THOUGHT YOU SAID. NOW, IF YOU'D JUST SIGN HERE...

NO, YOU DON'T UNDERSTAND. I'M QUITE SERIOUS. IF YOU WON'T TELL ME WHAT *INSTANT SLUDGE* IS FOR I WON'T SELL MY HOUSE

BUT, MY DEAR CHAP, HOW NAIVE CAN YOU GET? IT'S NOT FOR ANYTHING. PEOPLE JUST BUY IT

BUT THAT'S RIDICULOUS! I MEAN, WHY DO THEY? WHAT DO THEY DO WITH IT WHEN THEY'VE BOUGHT IT?

WHATEVER THEY LIKE. ALL ITS CONSTITUENTS ARE GUARANTEED ABSOLUTELY INNOCUOUS

YOU'RE JOKING. THIS HUGE BUILDING CAN'T BE A MONUMENT TO NOTHING. I'M GOING TO FIND OUT

MEMO, ALL DEPARTMENTS— FOREIGN BODY LOOSE IN THE ORGANISATION. DO NOT OBSTRUCT BUT RENDER NO ASSISTANCE. TIME IS MOTION. MOTION, TIME. OVER AND OUT

...AND SCOOP SAYS *INSTANT SLUDGE* ISN'T FOR ANYTHING. HE CAN'T MEAN IT. I MEAN, WHY WOULD PEOPLE BUY IT?

PERHAPS IT'S BECAUSE IT SAYS 'SAVE TWOPENCE NOW' ON A TICKET STUCK TO THE SIDE

TOP EXECUTIVES LIVE AT THE TOP OF BUILDINGS. THAT'S AS RIGID A BUSINESS PRINCIPLE AS BOILERMEN HAUNTING BASEMENTS

THERE'S ONLY ONE BUTTON FOR ALL THESE LIFTS. I WONDER WHICH WILL ARRIVE FIRST

YES, HERE WE ARE. I CAN SMELL THE CIGARS

INDOOR JUNGLES LTD

THIS LOT'S FOR THE MANAGING DIRECTOR'S OFFICE, AIN'T IT?

IDEA!

FOLLOW THEM AND DO WHAT I DO, RUFUS

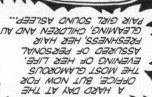

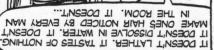

NO MEWS IS GOOD MEWS
April 1961

have got nearer to the plastic flesh and fake fibres of those years than any other cartoon-commentators alive.

That they entertain and delight, while remaining serious artists in this format, is not easy, and should not pass unacknowledged. Nor, indeed, should the unique qualities of Flook and Rufus, as seen in the context of the world they show us. They are often its victims, as we all are, but neither of them are innocents. Flook himself, like most of us, is a self-indulgent opportunist, though he is burdened with a conscience and has a deadly eye for the phoney. Indeed, apart from his looks and lack of inches, he is the kind of being I would really quite like to be—modest, gregarious, quick of wit and mind, with a first-name entry to circles high and low, a confidant of the Establishment, the Arts and the Stews, an adroit intriguer, always one step ahead of change, yet not entirely cynical or blasé—ever ready to be stung into protest or to join the side of the angels so long as he doesn't have to do it in the street and frighten the police-horses. I like Flook's knowledgeable calm, his unshockability, but also his occasional flickers of anger in the face of a bonehead bureaucracy. I like, too, his tolerance, his lack of malice, and resigned acceptance of constant betrayals by his friends. Flook sometimes drinks too much, and often exploits Rufus; but then Rufus exploits him too. Rufus is no fool, and although he may sometimes have to 'act-the-Alice' so that his simple questions may illuminate some scene, in his relationship with Flook he has a kind of feminine guile and durability, and generally knows where his next ice cream is coming from.

But in the main, Flook and Rufus are floating on a raft together, and the wealth of the strip lies in the shoals of characters that wash around them, some regularly recurring like circling sharks or dolphins, or flotsam dredged from the depths of dream. For us, Trog and Melly have hooked and played these in the whirlpool, and one must salute some of the most constant and memorable catches: Cordite-Smith and his Memsahib; Muckybrass and Bodger (those twin wide-boys of politics and poolroom); Pru Super-Groovy and her Chelsea Scoop; Jabb, the sponge-nose scavenger of Fleet Street; and all those itchy-bitchy *verités*, so closely observed and heard, thrown up for a moment and seldom seen again—medalled-doorkeepers, dew-lipped dollies, clerks and coppers; and all the humble, interlocking, selfseeking scoundrels of progress; and behind them the vast yawn of the working classes. (Indeed, if I may say so, when it comes to delineating the Common Man, Trog and Melly's sentimentalism is equalled only by Shakespeare's.)

Then take up this book, and you will see the scene of the Sixties, its characters already fretting and fading around you. . . . But for my part, if I might be allowed to choose from among my many favourites, they would be those Three who don't seem to fit in anywhere. Namely: Lucretia Bodger; Gob, her feline familiar; and, dearest to my heart, the Great Goat of Clapham.

LAURIE LEE

Flook's eye view of the Sixties is more than a comment on a period, or a scrapbook of contemporary follies; it is chiefly the celebration of a partnership as close as shared wit, hard labour, midnight oil and argument, and the stereo-vision of two separate but complementary talents can make it. To choose any ten years to represent an epoch is, of course, like choosing ten yards of water to represent a river. All the same, in this book you will find the Sixties sliced into four sharp strips as acrid and pungent as four squares of hot pizza. Or to change the metaphor again—four hot gospels of the decade, their themes disguised to the extent that no-one who lived through them will need an interpreter.

And this, I suppose, is one of the special qualities of Flook: our instant recognition of the scene he gives us, his brevity of signals leading to the heart of the matter—also effervescence mixed with a dash of bitters. For whatever his kiddy charms may have been in his far-off furry days, Flook is now about as cuddly as a wire-wool brush. A social cleanser, perhaps—though never self-righteous—a scourer of the fatuous, infamous fads of our time. It is here, I think, that the Trog-Melly technique works with such splendid laceration, carrying with it as many cutting-edges as an electric razor.

Visually, Flook and Rufus seem to have been kept deliberately low-keyed and neutral, the better to show off the magnificent pack of odds and sods they meet with. Over their years together, Trog and George Melly have caught, isolated, and fixed in the formaldehyde of news-print, a whole pantheon of contemporary creeps. Ranging from dotty duke to raw-toothed docker, each type is presented to us live by Trog's incisive, often acid-biting, line, by his eye for the familiar yet mythical face and posture; and also by George Melly's astounding, resounding ear—not only for accent, tone, tribal and regional rhythms, but again for the nuances of class and professional in-fighting, the trendy phrase that by-passes all understanding, the infinite shades of spite and aggression that the British can pack into the word 'sir', and the way in which Melly can send up a whole balloon of social vacuities in a sentence.

We are all of us in Flook; no-one is spared or favoured. Peers, proles, pinkies, powellites, right, left, and centre, no-one is allowed to escape—we are all of us paraded, day by day, to be punctured with the same ruthless and affectionate pleasure. Wherein, I suppose, lies the therapy of the thing: to have ourselves and our neighbours cut down to manageable size, like toast, at least once a morning.

Flook's eye view of the Sixties is the real hard stuff; there is no shandy or soda-pop here. The four story-strips preserved in these pages—and praise and thanks are due to the preserver—are brilliant glass-etched fantasies laid on a bed-rock of truth, and say about all ye need to know of that time. It was in many ways a sick and grasping decade, though it had its welcome frou-frous and liberations, and I believe that Trog and Melly, while keeping their lightness of touch,

INTRODUCTION

Choosing a daily newspaper is like choosing a local pub. More important than the indistinguishable layout will be the flavour of the contributors, or regulars. A paper, like a pub, will have its saloon-bar bores, hectoring politicos, sporty heavies, twittering babyshams. But occasionally, if you're lucky, you'll find in some accustomed snug or corner that rare spirit whose presence will lace your sanatized drink with the veritable kick of life; and it is for quite a while now that I have been going to the *Daily Mail* mainly for my diurnal intake of Flook.

Like many a maverick or changeling with a self-directing destiny, Flook had a peculiarly abstract conception. In fact, he was sired by Lord Rothermere out of Early Post-War Jazz (and few beginnings could be more abstract than that).

Briefly, the genesis was this. In 1948, while on a visit to America, Lord Rothermere saw a comic strip in a New York daily about a little boy with a magic uncle. He thought that his paper might carry something similar, but with an Anglo-Saxon twist—say, about a little boy with a magic pet. The *Mail* produced a synopsis called "Leftie and the Goop"; staffman Humphrey Lyttelton chopped 'Goop' into Flook'; colleague Trog (Wally Fawkes) set himself to drawing the pictures, and the strip was christened "Rufus" instead of the more provocative "Leftie".

It is now perhaps poignant to recall that for the first months of their life, little hero-boy Rufus and his roly-poly friend led a wispy whimsical relationship whose adventures were aimed solely at children. But, ah, for lost innocence—after a series of story-writers (including Sir Compton Mackenzie and godfather Lyttelton himself) a nursery revolution took place in which Flook slowly and subtly transformed himself from that cuddly little fur-ball, Rufus's toy-town plaything, into the disenchanted enchanter we all know today, the prod-nosed putter-down of our split-level society.

This year, 1970, marks the strip's coming of age; Flook and Rufus have now reached their majority. Trog has drawn them, and their world, during the whole of that time; while for the last fourteen years (expertly rocking the cradle of our TV/Bingo civilization) the stories and dialogue have been the result of the delicately tuned-in contributions of Trog's confederate musician, jazz-singer and writer George Melly.

First published 1970

Copyright © 1970 Associated Newspapers Limited

SBN 283 48423 3

Printed in Great Britain by
Thomas Nelson (Printers) Ltd
London and Edinburgh
for Sidgwick and Jackson Limited
1 Tavistock Chambers, Bloomsbury Way
London, W.C.1

FLOOK

A Flook's-eye View of the Sixties

by TROG

with an Introduction by
LAURIE LEE

SIDGWICK & JACKSON : LONDON

FLOOK

A Merry Christmas '70